Japanese Americans

Dale Anderson

Curriculum Consultant: Michael Koren,
Social Studies Teacher, Maple Dale School, Fox Point, Wisconsin

WORLD ALMANAC® LIBRARY

Please visit our web site at: www.garethstevens.com
For a free color catalog describing World Almanac® Library's
list of high-quality books and multimedia programs,
call 1-800-848-2928 (USA) or 1-800-387-3178 (Canada).
World Almanac® Library's fax: (414) 332-3567.

Library of Congress Cataloging-in-Publication Data

Anderson, Dale, 1953-
    Japanese Americans / by Dale Anderson.
        p. cm. – (World Almanac Library of American immigration)
    Includes bibliographical references and index.
    ISBN-10: 0-8368-7313-0 – ISBN-13: 978-0-8368-7313-9 (lib. bdg.)
    ISBN-10: 0-8368-7326-2 – ISBN-13: 978-0-8368-7326-9 (softcover)
    1. Japanese Americans–History–Juvenile literature.   2. Japanese Americans–
Social conditions–Juvenile literature.   3. Immigrants–United States–History–
Juvenile literature.   4. Japan–Emigration and immigration–History–Juvenile
literature.   5. United States–Emigration and immigration–History–Juvenile
literature.   I. Title.   II. Series.
    E184.J3A58   2007
    973'.004956–dc22   2006005325

First published in 2007 by
World Almanac® Library
A member of the WRC Media Family of Companies
330 West Olive Street, Suite 100
Milwaukee, WI 53212, USA

Copyright © 2007 by World Almanac® Library.

Produced by Discovery Books
Editor: Sabrina Crewe
Designer and page production: Sabine Beaupré
Photo researcher: Sabrina Crewe
Maps and diagrams: Stefan Chabluk
Consultant: Masako Nakamura
Gareth Stevens editorial direction: Mark J. Sachner
Gareth Stevens editor: Carol Ryback
Gareth Stevens art direction: Tammy West
Gareth Stevens production: Jessica Morris

Picture credits: CORBIS: cover, 8, 13, 14, 21, 24, 33, 35, 36, 42, 43; Library of
Congress: 10, 18, 22, 27, 28, 30, 31; Nagareda Studio: 41; New York Public Library:
7; Powell Tribune/Justin R. Lessman: 34; San Francisco History Center, San Francisco
Public Library: 17, 19; San Jose Taiko: title page; U.S. National Archives and Records
Adminsitration: 5, 29.

Printed in the United States of America

1 2 3 4 5 6 7 8 9 10 09 08 07 06

Contents

Front cover: During World War II, thousands of Japanese Americans were held in camps by the U.S. government. Unable to attend their own graduation in the 1940s, these Californians received their diplomas at the 2004 graduation ceremonies of their former high school.

Title page: Members of San Jose Taiko play *taiko* during a street performance in California in 2005. The taiko, or great drum, is a traditional Japanese instrument that has become popular in the United States.

Introduction

The United States has often been called "a nation of immigrants." With the exception of Native Americans— who have inhabited North America for thousands of years— all Americans can trace their roots to other parts of the world.

Immigration is not a thing of the past. More than seventy million people came to the United States between 1820 and 2005. One-fifth of that total —about fourteen million people—immigrated since the start of 1990. Overall, more people have immigrated permanently to the United States than to any other single nation.

Push and Pull

Historians write of the "push" and "pull" factors that lead people to emigrate. "Push" factors are the conditions in the homeland that convince people to leave. Many immigrants to the United States were—and still are—fleeing persecution or poverty. "Pull" factors are those that attract people to settle in another country. The dream of freedom or jobs or both continues to pull immigrants to the United States. People from many countries around the world view the United States as a place of opportunity.

Building a Nation

Immigrants to the United States have not always found what they expected. People worked long hours for little pay, often doing jobs that others did not want to do. Many groups also endured prejudice.

"I'm happy that people . . . want to know about Japan. Because some people are thinking about Japan in different way, old-fashioned way. I like to tell the people about my country, about Japanese life. When I go back to visit Japan . . . I talk about . . . American life. I'm so happy with that—interpreting for Japanese and for American."

Keiko Grant, Japanese American who married a U.S. soldier and moved to the United States in 1955, speaking in the 1970s

In spite of these challenges, immigrants and their children built the United States of America, from its farms, railroads, and computer industries to its beliefs and traditions. They have enriched American life with their culture and ideas. Although they honor their heritage, most immigrants and their descendants are proud to call themselves Americans first and foremost.

Immigrants from Japan

More than half a million people have come to the United States from Japan. First were the farm workers, mostly men, who came in the late 1800s. Females arriving in the early 1900s to become wives of these workers comprised most of the second wave. The third wave, from the late 1940s to the mid-1960s, included mainly women who had married members of the U.S. armed forces. The fourth wave, made up of single people and families, began in the 1970s and continues today.

Japanese Americans endured more discrimination than most other groups. For several decades, the United States banned all Asians from entering the country. Those already here were denied basic rights, including the opportunity to become U.S. citizens. During World War II—when the United States fought Japan—many

Americans of Japanese heritage were forced to leave their homes and live in prison-like internment camps. This experience had a profound effect on the whole Japanese American community.

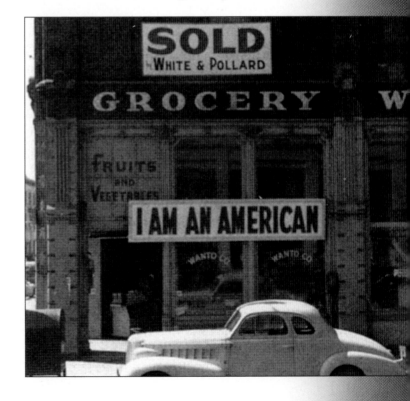

▶ The owners of this store in Oakland, California, were sent to an internment camp in 1942. Before they left, they placed a sign on their building to let people know that their Japanese heritage did not prevent them from being loyal Americans.

CHAPTER 1

Life in
the Homeland

The nation of Japan comprises several islands in the western Pacific Ocean. Its location has played a key part in Japan's development. Surrounded by water, the nation was separated from other nations and civilizations, and the Japanese people developed a unique society and culture.

Japanese Culture

This isolation was not complete, however. Centuries ago, people traveled by sea between Japan and China. Impressed by Chinese practices and ideas, the Japanese adopted some parts of Chinese culture, making use of what fit with their own customs and beliefs.

Japanese culture differs from European and American culture in many ways. American culture in particular puts great value on the individual. Japanese culture values the group, both the family group and society as a whole.

◀ Japan is an Asian country in the Pacific Ocean, situated near the coast of China. Japan is made up of several islands. Honshu and Hokkaido are the two largest islands.

RUSSIA

CHINA

Hokkaido

Sea
of
Japan

NORTH KOREA

SOUTH KOREA

Yellow
Sea

J A P A N

Hiroshima

Kyoto

Honshu

Tokyo ★

Shikoku

PACIFIC

OCEAN

Nagasaki   Kyushu

R Y U K Y U   I S L A N D S

Okinawa

200 miles
200 kilometers

N

JAPAN

★ Capital city
● City

▲ Japanese women in traditional **kimonos** serve tea in the late 1800s. Several
Japanese rituals and ceremonies include serving tea.

Head of the Household

Traditionally, males held the highest position in Japanese families.
The eldest male—the head of the family—owned and controlled
family property. When the family sat down to eat, he was served
first and always given the choicest pieces of food. He made family
decisions and was the person who dealt with other families—for
instance, in arranging marriages. Possible marriage partners were
thoroughly investigated before a match was approved.

Sons and Daughters

Sons were valued because they carried on the family name and
honor. When a father died, the eldest son took his position as
head of the family. Younger sons had a much lower social position
and often left the family household to start families of their own.

Daughters had less value because they could not carry on the
family line. Once they married, they joined their husband's family.
That put them under the rule of their husband's mother, a fate
many found difficult. Daughters-in-law were given the hardest
work to do. They were expected to awaken before the rest of the
family and immediately begin preparing meals, cleaning, and
doing other household chores. They continued working all day
and evening, only finishing after everyone else had gone to bed.

Politeness and a Sense of Honor

Social relations in Japan were formal and restrained. Husbands and
wives did not show open affection for one another, even within the

▲ In the 1800s, Japan was farmed mostly by peasants who lived in poverty. Peasant farmers, mostly from southern Japan, formed the first wave of emigration.

"The last time I was in Japan, my mother's friend visited me. I asked her if she wanted a cup of tea, and she said, 'Oh no,' so I thought she didn't want it, so did not serve anything. Then my mother came and said, 'Setsuko, you have to ask more. . . . And if someone says no, you better bring her a cup of tea anyway.' [In the United States] if someone says yes, it means yes. If someone says no, it means no."

Setsuko K., Japanese American who came to the United States in the 1970s, comparing Japanese and American culture in the late 1980s

family. People did not often speak directly about their feelings or needs. Being polite was and still is very important.

Other values underlie Japanese culture. When they ran into problems, Japanese people were expected to persevere without complaining. They had a deep sense of duty—to the family and the community. They also had a profound sense of personal, family, and national honor. Children were taught to act appropriately and do nothing that might bring dishonor on the family name. Many of these values are still important in Japan and among Japanese Americans today.

Japanese Religions

Most Japanese followed one of two religions. Shinto developed in ancient Japan and emphasized the following of rituals and visiting shrines. It did not have a formal church structure or priests. People carried out their practices on their own. Shinto fell into decline until the late 1800s, when Japan's ruler made it the official national religion. The other religion was Buddhism, which reached Japan from China. As practiced in Japan, Buddhism also calls for several rituals.

Opening Trade

When European explorers reached Japan during the 1500s and early 1600s, Japanese rulers permitted only limited trade. After 1639, contact was limited to Dutch traders, and even they were only allowed to do business from one Japanese port. For the next two centuries, Japan had little contact with the Western world.

That situation changed in 1853, when U.S. naval officer Matthew Perry arrived with four well-armed ships. Faced with superior military power and the unspoken threat of attack, Japan agreed in 1854 to open its doors to contact with the United States.

Japan Modernizes

In 1868, the emperor Meiji took power in Japan. He was determined to make the nation more modern. He invited experts from Europe and the United States to the islands to teach the Japanese about new technologies. The government sent students to colleges abroad to learn Western ways and bring back that knowledge to Japan. Japan began building factories and railroads. Eager to show it could be as strong as Western nations, Japan also built a large modern army and navy.

A small number of landowners controlled almost all the land in Japan as well as the lives of the poor peasants who farmed it. In 1873, the ruling Meiji government abolished this feudal system. The government also taxed landowners, using this money to fund its military and other programs.

Reasons to Leave

All these changes had a dramatic effect on Japanese society. Peasants, for the first time, could buy land, although most did not have the money to do so. Those that did faced high taxes and rising prices, and within a few years, many people lost the land they had so

Baseball in Japan

Among the features of Western life the Japanese adopted enthusiastically was the U.S. sport of baseball. First introduced in Japan in the 1870s, the game spread quickly through the country's schools. Intense fan interest led to the creation of a Japanese professional league in the 1930s. In recent years, several Japanese players have come to the U.S. major leagues. Ichiro Suzuki of the Seattle Mariners and Hideki Matsui of the New York Yankees proved that Japanese players have mastered the American game.

recently purchased. Some moved to cities, hoping to find work in factories. Manufacturing work was grueling, however, and wages were low. Conditions were especially poor in southern Japan.

In the 1880s, most people who left Japan in search of better lives came from this southern region. They could not leave, however, without the government's permission. The 1639 law that blocked foreigners from entering Japan also barred any Japanese from leaving the country. The government finally lifted that ban in 1885.

Growth and Conflict

Over the decades, Japan's economy improved, and it continued to modernize. From 1904 to 1905, Japan showed its military strength by easily defeating Russia in a brief war between the two nations.

▲ After the Japanese attack on Pearl Harbor, Hawaii, in 1941, U.S. sailors in small vessels approach the burning USS *West Virginia* to fight the flames. The attack brought the United States into World War II, leading to terrible suffering for Japanese Americans.

In the 1930s, much of the world was thrown into the economic collapse called the Great Depression. In Japan, top military leaders pushed civilians out of the government and took control. The new leaders wanted Japan to extend its power to other lands. In 1931, Japanese forces invaded China, a move that led to growing tension with the United States and Britain. Those nations placed an embargo on trade with Japan. Since Japan had to import oil and other vital supplies, the embargo threatened to cripple its economy.

World War II

Japan struck back. On December 7, 1941, Japanese military planes attacked the

> "It was a horrible shock, a terrible shock. We all thought there was no more Hiroshima, you see. That it was all burnt down. And it must be 50 percent of the people in this area, the Japanese in this area [of the United States], come from Hiroshima."
>
> *Hiroshi Yamada, who emigrated from Japan in 1901, remembering the Japanese American reaction to the 1945 bombing of Hiroshima*

U.S. naval base at Pearl Harbor, Hawaii. Japan also launched attacks against many U.S., British, and other military bases across the Pacific. The next day, the United States declared war on Japan. World War II—which had begun in Europe in 1939—reached the Pacific Ocean.

The war in the Pacific continued for four long years. The number of casualties was high on both sides as U.S. troops landed on islands the Japanese had seized and fought to oust the Japanese forces there. Meanwhile, U.S. airplanes bombarded Japanese cities with thousands of tons of bombs.

By the summer of 1945, U.S. forces had made their way to the shores of Japan. Military leaders planned an invasion of Japan, but they feared that such an effort would cost huge numbers of American lives. U.S. president Harry S. Truman decided instead to use a new weapon—the atomic bomb. In August of 1945, U.S. planes dropped a single bomb on each of the cities of Hiroshima and Nagasaki, instantly killing tens of thousands of people. The Japanese government surrendered.

Japan After the War

After the war, U.S. troops occupied Japan until 1952. The Japanese wrote a constitution that replaced the military leaders with an elected government and began to rebuild its devastated cities and factories. The United States gave aid to the rebuilding effort.

By the 1960s, Japan had rebounded. It had one of the world's fastest-growing economies. By the early 1970s, Japan's automobile manufacturers and makers of electronic goods were beginning to sell their products in large quantities all over the world.

National economic growth led to personal prosperity. The Japanese people led comfortable lives, with plenty of luxury goods to enjoy. Relations between the United States and Japan became close, although the two countries often disagreed on trade issues. The Japanese adopted aspects of Western culture, just as they had once acquired pieces of Chinese culture.

CHAPTER 2

Emigration

Soon after Japan's government lifted the ban on travel to other countries, emigration began. Poor farmers left Japan, hoping to work abroad for a few years and save enough money so they could return home and buy land in Japan. Early in 1885, a ship from Japan reached Hawaii carrying nearly one thousand Japanese workers. This trip marked the beginning of Japanese immigration to the United States—although until 1898, Hawaii was an independent kingdom.

Over the next forty years, about two hundred thousand Japanese workers came to Hawaii. By the early 1900s, many Japanese were traveling not only to Hawaii but also to the United States mainland.

The Government Role

From 1885 to the early 1900s, the Japanese government encouraged emigration to relieve the social tension caused by economic problems at home. The government also hoped that supplying workers would help build good relations with other countries. The government allowed the formation of local emigration companies to process people departing from specific regions of Japan.

Local government officials decided who was allowed to emigrate, following strict rules set by the national government. The government favored sending males between the ages of twenty-five and thirty who were experienced farmers and had completed their required military service. The men had to be single or, if married, without children. They had to be healthy and willing to work hard. Each also had to find two or three people who owned property to sign a guarantee that the emigrant was of good character and would stay at his job.

Financing the Trip

Many Japanese peasants who wanted to emigrate could not afford to pay for the journey. Some borrowed money from family members or from local business people. Others pooled their resources, using their cash to send one member of a group, who began working in Hawaii or the United States. He sent money back to the group in Japan, where it was kept until there was enough to send the next member of the group. Then both he and the first emigrant sent back money, so a third could buy a ticket. In this way, the whole group managed to emigrate.

A large number of emigrants financed the trip by signing labor contracts. In this case, a hiring agent paid their passage. He was repaid—with interest—from the workers' wages. In their labor contracts, the workers agreed to work for three to five years.

Crossing the Pacific

On the ocean voyage to Hawaii or the United States, emigrants were crowded into a large compartment on a ship that had few or no windows and little fresh air. Some had no bunks; the travelers had to sleep on the floor. Food was poor and sparse, and many passengers became seasick. It could take as long as four weeks to complete the crossing to the United States. The journey to Hawaii took less time, but traveling conditions were equally unpleasant.

The Women of the Second Wave

In 1908, the United States and Japan reached an agreement to end the emigration of Japanese laborers to the United States. The wives of men already living in the United States were allowed to join them, however, and nearly seventy thousand Japanese women emigrated to the United States between 1908 and 1921.

Some Japanese American men returned to Japan to marry and then recrossed the Pacific with their new wives. Many women came as "picture brides." The name came from the fact

▼ Between 1908 and 1921, thousands of Japanese women emigrated to the United States during the second wave of emigration. These immigrants arrived by ship in San Francisco, California, in 1920.

13

"I believe we all go to America for one of the following reasons:
1. Hopes of becoming rich.
2. Curiosity of this civilized country called America.
3. Fear of mother-in-law in Japan.
4. Anxiety in those who have passed marriage age.
5. Dreams of an idyllic, romantic life in the new land.
6. Lack of ability to support self.
7. Sacrificing self to obey parents' wishes."

Shika Takaya, a picture bride who came to the United States in 1917

▲ A newly married couple presents papers to a U.S. official in Tokyo, Japan, in 1951. U.S. laws passed in the 1940s allowed the Japanese brides of U.S. servicemen to emigrate to the United States.

that Japanese American men started the marriage process by sending a photograph of themselves back to Japan. A marriage was arranged in Japan and took place in the husband's absence. The government then gave the picture bride a passport and she boarded a ship to cross the ocean and join her new husband.

Many of these brides made the ocean crossing together. The daughter of one picture bride related what life was like on these ships: "[Mother] met a dozen or so other picture brides, and the kimono-clad young women compared photos of their future husbands, discussing their anxieties, sometimes joking uneasily about their future."

Military Brides Leave Japan

After World War II came the third wave of Japanese emigration to the United States: military brides, sometimes called "war brides." These women married U.S. soldiers and sailors who served in Japan. The picture brides had been supported by their families in the decision to leave, but that was not always the case with military brides. Many families tried to convince their daughters not to marry. They worried about cultural differences and about the fact that their daughters would be moving far away. Some families actually shunned their daughters. Others reluctantly allowed the marriage to take place. Military brides were looked down on by Japanese

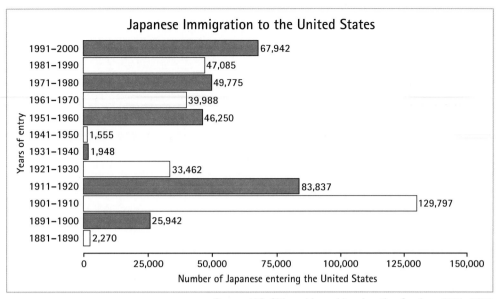

Japanese Immigration to the United States

Years of entry	Number of Japanese entering the United States
1991–2000	67,942
1981–1990	47,085
1971–1980	49,775
1961–1970	39,988
1951–1960	46,250
1941–1950	1,555
1931–1940	1,948
1921–1930	33,462
1911–1920	83,837
1901–1910	129,797
1891–1900	25,942
1881–1890	2,270

Source: U.S. Citizenship and Immigration Services, 1881–2000

▲ This chart shows how Japanese immigration was high in the early 1900s and then rose again after World War II. Today, on average, about eight thousand Japanese immigrants arrive annually.

society as a whole. Many Japanese could not accept the women marrying men from what had been an enemy nation. Others disapproved because the marriages were not traditionally arranged.

Japanese Emigration Today

In the 1970s, many Japanese companies began launching business operations in the United States. They sent—and continue to send—executives and managers from Japan to the United States to join those operations. Others leave Japan to attend college or graduate school in the United States. Many Japanese people emigrate to the United States because they have married or intend to marry a U.S. citizen.

Immigrants who are not marrying U.S. citizens must obtain work or student visas to be allowed to enter the United States. The visas say that they can only stay for a fixed amount of time—a few years, usually. Thousands of these Japanese people have returned to Japan. Many, however, have stayed and become U.S. citizens.

The fourth wave of immigration, which began in the 1970s, has brought more equal numbers of males and females. Some of those new Japanese Americans are women with good education who feel that they cannot advance professionally in Japan. Although the women have college degrees, Japanese companies still favor men. Many Japanese women believe they will find better opportunities working in the United States.

Arriving in the United States

While the United States is a nation of immigrants, it has not always welcomed new arrivals. For many years, people coming from Asia were especially unwelcome. Tens of thousands of Chinese workers emigrated to the West Coast from about 1850 to the early 1880s. White American workers developed intense hostility toward the Chinese, and those feelings were later directed at Japanese immigrants.

Arriving in Hawaii

The movement of Japanese workers to Hawaii and the United States in the late 1800s was well organized. Fifty or so U.S. companies recruited workers in Japan to work on sugarcane plantations they owned on the island. Those workers were moved in large numbers to their destinations. Once they arrived, company agents met them, handed out work assignments, and sent the workers wherever they were supposed to go.

On the West Coast

On the United States mainland, workers went to farms, fisheries, and railroad and lumber industries. Most Japanese American immigrants in the late 1800s and early 1900s arrived in Seattle, Washington. That changed in 1910, when the government opened a new West Coast immigration station on Angel Island, in San Francisco Bay in California. All Asian immigrants were then sent through Angel Island, a process that could involve days or even weeks of detention.

Prejudice and Foreign Relations

Prejudice against Japanese immigrants appeared from the start, and it increased as their numbers grew. In 1892, San Francisco's board of education ruled that Japanese American students in the city had

▲ Angel Island detainees play baseball in the 1930s while they wait to be processed. Angel Island in San Francisco Bay, California, was the site of the West Coast's major processing center for Asian immigrants from 1900 to 1940.

to attend the schools set aside for Chinese American students. A Japanese diplomat working in the city protested and was able to get the board to reverse the decision.

In 1901, California's governor asked Congress to pass a law banning Japanese immigration. Congress did not act, however. Japan was a strong nation, and it had a supporter in the White House. Theodore Roosevelt, who became president in 1901, wanted good relations with Japan, and he opposed any laws that would upset Japan's government.

In 1906, a situation arose in San Francisco that brought the issue to a head. The San Francisco board of education once again issued an order for Japanese American children to attend the city's

Japanese Association of America

The Japanese government kept an eye on the treatment of its people in other lands and stepped in to object to any unfair treatment. It also helped launch the Japanese Association of America, formed in 1908 to aid Japanese immigrants. The association handled the legal details of the immigration of wives and children, for instance. It recorded the marriages, births, and deaths of Japanese Americans and represented the immigrants with U.S. political and business leaders. The association also urged Japanese Americans to adopt U.S. culture and educate their children. Japan hoped to prove to the United States that Japanese people could be desirable members of society. Those goals became an important part of Japanese American life.

SAN FRANCISCO'S MAYOR WANTS
EXCLUSION ACT TO BAR THE JAPS

EUGENE E. SCHMITZ, LABOR CHAMPION, REGARDS THEM AS A FAR GREATER MENACE THAN THE CHINESE.

By E. C. Leffingwell.
Special Correspondence of the Newspaper Enterprise Association.
San Francisco, March 00.—"I would sooner see the bars of civilization let down on this western borderland to the heathen Chinese, and meet all of the grave dangers incidental to their coming, than to wit-

regard," he said, when asked to express his views, "because the public health must be safeguarded above all things, and the hand of the law must be left free and powerful in this regard.

"Here in San Francisco the Board

"With great pride of race, [the Japanese] have no idea of assimilating in the sense of amalgamation [becoming one society]. They do not come to this country with any desire or any intent to lose their racial or national identity. They come here specifically and professedly for the purpose of colonizing and establishing here permanently the proud [Japanese] race. They never cease to be Japanese."

Newspaper owner Valentine Stuart McClatchy, 1924

▲ Prejudice originally directed at Chinese Americans was extended to Japanese immigrants by the early 1900s. This 1905 publication quotes the views of San Francisco's mayor, who wanted a total ban on Japanese immigration.

segregated Chinese schools. Roosevelt worked out a settlement, and the children were allowed to attend white schools. In return, Japan agreed not to allow any more Japanese men to come to the United States. The arrangement went into effect in 1908. This "Gentlemen's Agreement," as it was called, sharply cut Japanese immigration.

The Picture Brides Arrive

The Gentlemen's Agreement allowed in wives of Japanese men already in the United States, and the picture brides began to arrive. On arrival, the picture brides had several shocks. First, the marriage that had taken place in Japan was not recognized by the U.S. government until 1917. Before that year, bride and groom had to undergo a U.S. wedding ceremony. Often, the marriage took place as soon as the women reached the shore.

⌃ Japanese women gather around a table during the arrival process at Angel Island. To the Japanese picture brides who arrived to join their husbands in California in the early 1900s, everything was new and strange.

Other surprises included meeting their new husbands. As immigrant Shika Takaya later recalled, "Men who claimed to be owners of large stores turned out to be running small fruit stands. Big farmers turned out to [have only] five or six acres." Some women cried when they realized that their husbands were much older than their pictures had shown them to be. The gap in age between husband and wife was often fifteen years or so.

Culture Shock

Like most immigrants, the picture brides also felt culture shock. They were startled and upset by the sharp differences between U.S. and Japanese culture. The food, clothing, and homes they found were completely different from what they had known in Japan. One picture bride remembered being shocked to be fed meat still attached to the bone. In Japan, she had only eaten thinly sliced meat.

Those who lived in Japanese American communities could often rely on the help and

"Mother . . . was pleased to see Father standing straight and tall with lots of hair. The picture that she brought with her had not deceived her. In fact he was quite handsome. And he seemed kind."

Grace Shibata, U.S.-born daughter of two immigrants, describing in the 1990s the favorable meeting of her picture bride mother and her father in the early 1900s

Becoming Citizens

For many years, the 1795 Naturalization Act set the rules for how foreign-born people could become U.S. citizens. It declared that only "free, white persons" had the right to do so. Asian immigrants were resident aliens, but they were not eligible for citizenship. Their children who were born on U.S. soil became citizens at birth, however.

A Japanese immigrant named Takao Ozawa challenged the naturalization law, but the U.S. Supreme Court ruled against him in 1922. Not until 1952 were Japanese immigrants given the right to become U.S. citizens. In the next thirty years, nearly fifty thousand Japanese Americans gained citizenship, finally achieving a long-sought goal.

companionship of other women who understood them. Those who lived in white American communities felt more isolated. Some had difficulty communicating with neighbors, while others had to face the hostile stares or taunts of prejudiced white Americans.

A Halt to Japanese Immigration

Some Americans protested the arrival of the picture brides, saying it violated Japan's promise to end immigration to the United States. In 1920, Japan stopped issuing passports to Japanese women. Then, in 1924, the National Origins Act barred any immigration by people "ineligible for citzenship." Under U.S. law at the time, this ban applied to most Asians. For the next twenty years or so, the number of people leaving Japan for the United States slowed to a trickle. In the 1930s, fewer than two hundred people, on average, arrived each year.

A Change in Immigration Laws

After World War II, U.S. immigration laws changed again. A law passed in 1947 allowed Japanese women who were married to members of the U.S. armed forces to enter the country. Then, the 1952 McCarran-Walter Act opened the door slightly to immigration from Japan and other Asian countries. In 1965, a new immigration law finally allowed widespread immigration from Asia.

Arriving After 1965

The business people, families, and students who came from Japan between the 1970s and the present differ from earlier groups in that they generally have more education. In addition, Japanese culture today is far more influenced by U.S. culture than was the case one hundred years earlier. As a result, many of these immigrants have

◀ Tatsumi Kimishima, shown here at the opening of Nintendo World in New York City in 2005, became president of Nintendo of America in 2002 after years of working for Japanese companies in the United States. Many business people come from Japan to New York and other U.S. cities as employees of Japanese companies.

some familiarity with U.S. ways of life and thinking before they arrive, and many already speak English. All of these factors make the experience of arriving in the United States and taking up residence a lot easier than it was for earlier arrivals.

Many of today's immigrants have the security of coming with or joining a spouse who is American. Others have talents or training that allow them to land good jobs in the United States. Ongoing business ties between the two nations support a continuing flow of business people, and Japanese students continue to enroll in U.S. colleges and universities. Many of these people, finding good opportunities, decide to stay permanently and make the United States their home.

The Generations

As a group, people of Japanese descent who live outside Japan are called Nikkei. When Japanese immigration was halted in the 1920s, the Nikkei community in the United States was limited to people from the first two waves of immigrants—the workers and their wives—and their descendants. The experience of each of these generations was unique, and Japanese Americans have given each a name:

Issei—(meaning first generation) were people born in Japan who emigrated to the United States and became the first generation of Japanese Americans.

Nisei—(second generation) are children born in the United States of Issei parents. The Nisei included many Kibei, children sent to Japan to be educated and who returned to the United States.

Sansei—(third generation) are the children of the Nisei.

Yonsei—(fourth generation) are the children of the Sansei.

Facing Prejudice and Internment

Between 1885 and 1924, about two hundred thousand Japanese people, mostly men, arrived to work in Hawaii. Slightly more than half worked only a few years and then returned to Japan. Tens of thousands of others remained or moved later to the United States mainland.

Life on Hawaii's Plantations

Japanese laborers worked long days, usually starting at 5:00 A.M. They were constantly under the watchful eye of a foreman, who would beat any worker he thought was not working hard enough. Workers who broke plantation rules were fined.

In the early years, men outnumbered the women more than thirteen to one, although that ratio changed later. The women did

▼ Japanese Americans had their own quarters on Hawaiian plantations, such as these buildings in Honolulu in the early 1900s. Plantation workers of the period were harshly treated by their employers.

much the same work as the men but were paid only three-quarters as much in wages. Along with farm work, women did the cooking, sewing, and laundry.

The plantations also had Chinese, Filipino, Korean, and other workers. Plantation owners assigned each group to its own housing and to particular areas of the plantation to work. The plantation owners paid the various groups different rates to keep them hostile to one another so they would not unite against their managers.

The Organic Act of 1900

Before 1900, many Japanese workers in Hawaii were bound by labor contracts. In 1900, Congress passed the Organic Act, which placed Hawaii officially under U.S. law and made labor contracts illegal.

The Organic Act had a profound effect on the Japanese American community. Since Japanese workers in Hawaii no longer had to fulfill their labor contracts, many left Hawaii for the mainland. Only about two thousand Japanese Americans lived on the mainland in 1890, but by 1920 that number topped 110,000. Nearly forty thousand of these Japanese Americans had moved to the mainland from Hawaii, while the rest had immigrated from Japan.

Settling on the West Coast

The vast majority of Japanese Americans settled on the West Coast. In 1920, two-thirds of all Japanese Americans lived in California. About sixty-five hundred were scattered throughout the northeastern states, the Midwest, and the South. Japanese Americans on the mainland worked a variety of jobs. They built railroads in Washington, fished or farmed in California, canned fish in Alaska, and dug coal in Wyoming.

Japanese American Farmers

Many Japanese Americans grew fruits, vegetables, and rice on farms. Japanese

"The first job I got was on the railroad in the state of Washington. . . . I didn't spend much money and I saved. And after about three years I went back to Japan to marry. . . . When I brought my wife over I didn't want to work on the railroad anymore, so I got a job in Seattle with an export-import company. . . . I worked first as a stock boy, loading, unloading things, and later in the office. I saved my money and then, after three or four years, I decided to set up my own business—a dry-cleaning business."

Taro Murata, who came from Japan in 1907 at age nineteen and settled in Washington, speaking in the late 1970s

American farmers were very successful because of their agricultural experience in Japan. They produced 10 percent of California's crops even though they owned only a fraction of the state's land. They introduced rice, celery, and strawberry production to California.

▼ A Japanese American farmer carries a crate of cauliflower on his California farm in 1942. Japanese immigrants brought their agricultural skills and hard work to California, transforming the farming industry there.

Because of white racism, however, several western states passed alien land laws. These laws banned aliens—which meant all Asian American immigrants—from owning land. Aliens were also prevented from signing a lease that lasted longer than three years.

Some Japanese Americans, frustrated and angered by these laws, moved to other states or returned to Japan. Others found ways around the laws. Issei parents bought land in the names of their Nisei children, who were citizens because they had been born in the United States. Some found white landowners who were willing to sign fair leases.

Living and Working in Cities

Over time, more Japanese Americans settled in cities. Their neighborhoods were often situated near the Chinatowns of such cities as San Francisco and Los Angeles in California and Seattle, Washington. Many city dwellers owned their own businesses. These were small-scale enterprises, such as laundry services, food stores, hotels, and barbershops. Because of discrimination, few Japanese Americans worked as wage earners in white-owned businesses.

Becoming Americans

The addition of wives in the 1910s transformed Japanese American society. Suddenly, the community had large numbers of families and children. With the birth of children, many Issei men began to put down roots in the new country.

The great majority of Japanese Americans married other Japanese Americans. A law passed by the federal government

Population Growth

Each year from 1913 to 1930 saw the birth of at least two thousand Japanese American children. In the heaviest years, those numbers soared to more than five thousand. The result was a population boom. The pattern of early Japanese immigration continued to influence population numbers for many years. From 1930 to 1950, the Japanese American population increased very slowly. Few immigrants were coming, and most of the Nisei had been born. Then the Nisei grew up and had their children in the same twenty-year period. The Japanese American population boomed again, boosted also by a period of increased immigration.

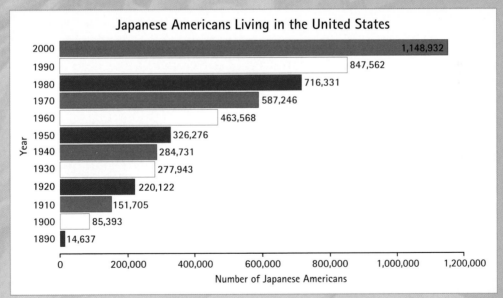

Japanese Americans Living in the United States

Year	Number of Japanese Americans
2000	1,148,932
1990	847,562
1980	716,331
1970	587,246
1960	463,568
1950	326,276
1940	284,731
1930	277,943
1920	220,122
1910	151,705
1900	85,393
1890	14,637

Source: U.S. Census Bureau, 1890–2000

This chart shows how the Japanese American population grew between 1890 and 2000. Based on the 2000 Census, the U.S. government estimated there were fourteen thousand unauthorized residents—people without visas or citizenship—of Japanese descent in the United States in that year.

in 1922 discouraged marriages with people from other groups. The Cable Act said that any U.S. woman who married an alien ineligible for citizenship would lose her own citizenship. This made it very unlikely that white women would marry Asian American men or that an Asian immigrant man could marry a U.S. citizen.

The Issei made an effort to adopt American ways of life. Encouraged by the Japanese Association, they wore Western-style clothing. Many learned English, either at work or by taking classes. Some men deliberately worked as servants in white homes to learn the language. Once they felt they knew enough English, they left to pursue other kinds of employment or set up businesses.

"The Issei mother announces that she has made a very simple dinner . . . but the children understand that she would say this even if she had been cooking for days beforehand. Her disclaimer is especially loud if there are visitors present."

Harry H. L. Kitano, Nisei anthropology professor, describing a Japanese American family meal in the early 1900s

The Nisei

Children learned English in school and adopted American ways more completely than their parents. These practices led to conflict within the family, as Nisei children often rejected their parents' culture. Many Nisei went by American first names at school, even though they answered to their Japanese first names at home. Religion joined language as an area of difference. Most Issei were Buddhists, while a large proportion of Nisei were Christians. Some Issei women became Christians as well because joining the churches helped them feel part of a larger community. In addition, these churches offered special services such as English classes and child care.

An Established Community

In 1930, the Japanese American Citizens League (JACL) formed to campaign on behalf of Japanese Americans. This group—organized by students—pushed the government to give citizenship to Issei who had joined the U.S. armed forces during World War I. It also pushed for repeal of the Cable Act that discouraged marriage with white Americans. Both campaigns eventually succeeded.

The JACL also urged Nisei to show loyalty to the United States and to adopt U.S. culture. That path, they hoped, would lead to greater acceptance. Some Nisei, however, were confused about their identity. They felt that they were neither American—because they were not accepted by whites—nor Japanese, because they had not been raised in Japan.

By the 1930s, the Japanese American community was firmly established. National and state laws had repeatedly denied or taken away the rights of Japanese Americans, but they still expressed loyalty to the United States.

Forced Removal from the West Coast

In spite of their patriotism and determination to be good, loyal Americans, Japanese Americans found their lives and communities shattered by events in World War II. After the 1941 attack on Pearl Harbor, U.S. leaders began expressing doubts—completely unfounded—about the loyalty of Japanese Americans. General John DeWitt, in charge of defending the West Coast, dismissed Japanese Americans' loyalty with the words, "a Jap is a Jap." Members of the U.S. military and Congress urged President Franklin D. Roosevelt to order the removal of Japanese Americans from the West Coast. In February 1942, Roosevelt issued Executive Order 9066. It allowed the army to exclude people from any area it judged necessary.

▶ A military police officer posts a notice announcing the removal of Japanese Americans from Bainbridge Island in Puget Sound, Washington, in 1942. Such notices were posted in communities all along the West Coast after the United States entered World War II.

▲ Japanese Americans load luggage onto a vehicle as they prepare to leave the Manzanar Relocation Center near Independence, California, for another internment camp somewhere in the West.

"To pack and evacuate in forty-eight hours was an impossibility. . . . Having had absolute confidence in democracy, I could not believe my very eyes what I had seen that day. America, the standard bearer of democracy, had committed the most heinous crime in its history."

Nisei Joe Kurihara, remembering in the 1990s his feelings when Japanese Americans were evacuated in the 1940s

A few weeks later, DeWitt declared that Japanese Americans would be evacuated forcibly and quickly from the West Coast. Forced to sell or abandon their property, Japanese Americans had no bargaining power. Whites streamed into Japanese American communities to buy homes and businesses at low prices.

Sent to the Camps

By the summer of 1942, all the West Coast evacuees had been placed in one of ten camps, called relocation camps, in western states or Arkansas. These camps were located in desolate, isolated areas such as deserts, mountainous regions, or swamps.

About 157,000 Japanese Americans lived on the U.S. mainland in 1940. About 120,000 —or about 75 percent of them—were forced to leave their homes and businesses for the camps. About two-thirds of these people were U.S. citizens. None of them was ever convicted of betraying the United States.

Life in the Camps

The internment camps were similar in some ways to prisons and in other ways to military bases. Families lived in buildings called barracks, long buildings divided into small units. Each family was given a space about 20 by 20 feet (6 by 6 meters). Each family unit had a wood-burning stove, a single electric light, and a cot for each person. The families in several buildings shared a large dining hall, a recreation hall, a laundry, and separate buildings for men's and women's bathroom facilities.

Sirens awoke people at 7:00 A.M. After camp officials took attendance, breakfast was served. Then children went to school and adults to jobs in the camps. After dinner, there was another roll call by camp officials, and then the Japanese Americans went back to their barracks. A curfew meant they could not be outside at night. U.S. soldiers patrolled the camps.

▶ High school students gather before class at Heart Mountain Relocation Center in Wyoming. Around them are buildings in which they live, eat, and study—all within the boundaries of a barbed-wire fence.

Fighting Internment

Some Japanese Americans fought internment, including Fred Korematsu, who took his case to the U.S. Supreme Court. In a six-to-three decision, the Supreme Court ruled in 1944 that the internment was legal because it was based on military necessity. The three justices who strongly disagreed with this decision were Owen Roberts, Frank Murphy, and Robert Jackson. They said that the internment had nothing to do with security but was based on discrimination and was therefore unconstitutional.

In another case decided in 1944, called *Ex Parte Endo,* the Supreme Court gave Japanese Americans their one legal victory. All nine justices agreed that Japanese Americans who were loyal citizens could

▼ During internment, these Japanese American farm workers, interned at the Manzanar camp in California, produced their own food.

not be held in the camps. The Nisei, at least, would have to be allowed to go home. The Supreme Court did not admit, however, that the wartime internment was unconstitutional. The same day, the U.S. military announced that the camps would be closed. It set a timetable of six months to one year.

Fighting for the United States

Several thousand Japanese Americans, meanwhile, fought for the United States in World War II. In January 1943, the U.S. Army asked in Hawaii for fifteen hundred Nisei volunteers. Nearly ten thousand men showed up. One of the volunteers, Minoru Hinahara, explained his thinking: "I wanted to . . . contribute to America. . . . My parents could not become citizens but they told me, 'You fight for your country.'" About twenty-six hundred of the Hawaiian volunteers were sent to the mainland to train with eight hundred Nisei from the internment camps. During World War II, a higher percentage of the Japanese American population entered the U.S. armed forces than any other ethnic group.

Many of these soldiers formed the 442nd Regimental Combat Team. After months of training, the unit was sent to Europe to fight. The soldiers performed brilliantly, and the 442nd received more honors and medals than any other unit its size.

> There were army-type barracks, with 200 to 205 people to each block. . . . It was all surrounded by barbed wire, and armed soldiers. I think they said only seven people were killed in total, though thirty were shot, because they went too close to the fence. Where we were, nobody thought of escaping because you'd be more scared of the swamps. . . ."
>
> *Nisei Yuri Kochiyama, speaking in the late 1980s, describing her wartime internment camp*

▲ The 442nd Regimental Combat Team, a unit of Japanese American soldiers, at Camp Shelby, Mississippi, in 1943. The 442nd fought on the battlefields of Europe, and its members became heroes of World War II.

CHAPTER 5

Building New Lives

After World War II, those Japanese Americans who had been placed in internment camps had to begin their lives anew. They were allowed to return to the West Coast, where a fortunate few had non-Japanese friends who gave them jobs or leased them land so they could farm. The great majority of Japanese Americans, however, had to rebuild their lives from nothing.

Starting to Rebuild

That process was made more difficult by lingering prejudice. Daniel Inouye (now a U.S. senator) was a captain in the 442nd Regimental Combat Team and lost an arm fighting for the United States. Yet a white barber in San Francisco, California, told him to leave his shop with the comment, "We don't serve Japs here"—even though Inouye was wearing his army uniform. Countless other Japanese Americans faced similar insults as well as difficulties in finding jobs and places to live because of white prejudice.

Many Nisei who had owned farmland had been forced to sell it in the rush of the evacuation, and the California government had seized the land of others. Some people had managed to keep hold of their land but found it overgrown when they returned. It took backbreaking work to make that farmland productive again.

"The only thing I was looking for was to work in a restaurant as a waitress. But I couldn't find anything. . . . As soon as they found out I was Japanese, they would say no. . . . For a while, I could last maybe two hours, and somebody would say, 'Is that a Jap?' And as soon as someone would ask that, the boss would say, 'Sorry, you gotta go. We don't want trouble here.'"

Nisei Yuri Kochiyama, recalling in the late 1980s her search for work in California after World War II

▲ Many Japanese Americans moved to Chicago, Illinois, and other large cities after World War II and did their best to become accepted by white Americans. The Terao family, shown here in 1946, bought a delicatessen and sold strictly kosher food to the Jewish community in their Chicago neighborhood.

Spreading Out

These challenges led many Japanese Americans to move away from the West Coast and into cities in other parts of the country. These Japanese Americans did not set up new ethnic communities, and they tended to settle away from existing ethnic neighborhoods. They tried instead to blend into white society, adopting aspects of U.S. culture in the hopes of gaining acceptance.

The number of Japanese Americans in communities across the nation grew. Ten times more Japanese Americans lived in Denver, Colorado, in 1950 than in 1940. New York City's Japanese American population increased by eight times. Chicago's increased from fewer than four hundred in 1940 to about eleven thousand in 1950.

Flourishing in Hawaii

Americans of Japanese descent living in Hawaii had an easier time. They had not been expelled from their homes, and Hawaiian society was more multiethnic than mainland society. Many veterans of the 442nd Regimental Combat Team went to college and started new careers. They became the dominant force in local politics and helped lead the effort to bring Hawaii to statehood in 1959.

Gaining Rights

After World War II, the United States saw an expansion of civil rights for various minority groups. New court decisions ended some of the unfair practices that had plagued Japanese Americans for decades. In 1948, the Supreme Court issued a ruling that weakened the alien land laws, which were finally declared unconstitutional four years later. That same year, 1952, the McCarran-Walter Act granted Japanese immigrants the right to become U.S. citizens. In 1967, the Supreme Court ruled that laws banning marriages between people of different races were unconstitutional.

Military Wives

While the Issei and Nisei tried to rebuild their lives, thousands of Japanese women were arriving to start new lives. Nearly fifty thousand Japanese women came to the United States between 1947 and

The Struggle for Redress

In 1948, Congress passed a law allowing Japanese Americans to make claims for property lost due to internment. The law put a cap of only $2,500 on the amount a person could claim, far below the losses Japanese Americans actually suffered. In the 1970s, Japanese Americans, with the support of the Asian American community and others, began pushing for redress. They

wanted an apology for internment as well as payments compensating Japanese Americans for their suffering. Congress finally passed the Civil Liberties Act of 1988. The law admitted that the internment was a "fundamental injustice" and apologized for the action. The bill also provided for payment of $20,000 to each internment camp survivor.

▶ Among those who worked for the Civil Liberties Act of 1988 were U.S. Senator Alan K. Simpson and U.S. Congressman Norman Mineta, seen here at a 2005 dedication ceremony at the former Heart Mountain internment camp. In the 1940s, Mineta was interned at the camp, while Simpson was growing up in nearby Cody, Wyoming. The two boys met, forming a friendship lasting more than sixty years.

1964 after marrying members of the U.S. armed forces. Prejudice against the wartime enemy was still strong, and military brides did not often find a warm welcome from soldiers' families and neighbors. Many of the brides had little contact with people who knew their language and culture. Military brides faced huge adjustments, especially when their marriages did not survive and they found themselves alone in U.S. society.

Changing Attitudes

As the decades passed, however, Japanese Americans saw attitudes toward them soften. Distance from the war made bitter feelings fade. The fact that Japan became a key ally of the United States also promoted wider acceptance of Japanese Americans. So did growing interest in Japanese culture in the late 1900s. Many Americans from other groups wanted to learn more about Buddhism and Japanese martial arts. Traditional Japanese food also gained in popularity in these decades.

Relations between Japanese Americans and whites did not always remain smooth, however. Trade conflicts between the United States and Japan

"My mom found ways not just to survive but also to keep alive her Japanese heritage in a very foreign land. When we moved to Maryland I remember literally hours she spent on the phone with Aiko and Akemi, friends who moved to America also. Circulating Japanese magazines amongst the Japanese girls. . . . Making long trips to the one Japanese market in the Washington area. Insisting on speaking Japanese to us kids. . . . Cooking [Japanese dishes] in between steak and potatoes."

American-born Kayla Brown, describing in 2000 the life of her mother, a Japanese military bride

▲ By the late 1900s, Americans were familiar with several aspects of Japanese culture. Japanese restaurants serving sushi (displayed above in Little Tokyo, Los Angeles) became especially popular.

often led to ill feelings toward the Japanese. That tension reached a height in the 1970s, when many American automobile workers lost their jobs as competition from Japanese car companies increased. Resentment over economic issues has declined since then. Another reason for lessened anti-Japanese feeling is that Japanese immigration to the United States has simply not been very large.

School and Work

From the start, the Japanese American community emphasized education. As a result, each generation of Japanese Americans went further in school than the previous one. Most Issei had an elementary school education, with perhaps some secondary school. Most Nisei had a high school diploma, and some had a college degree or at least a few years of college. The Sansei tended to have a bachelor's degree or a more advanced degree.

▲ Two Japanese American girls wore traditional kimonos to celebrate the cherry blossom season in 1967 in the Japanese Tea Gardens in San Mateo, California. Japanese Americans who arrived after World War II were more likely to express their Japanese heritage, and U.S. society became more accepting of different cultures.

More education led to better jobs. The Nisei were far more likely than their parents to have professional or technical jobs—as doctors or engineers, for example—or to work as managers. That was even more true for the Sansei.

Moving Away from Japanese Heritage

While the Nisei were far more American than the immigrant Issei, their children and grandchildren were even more so. Sansei enjoyed Japanese food and took part in Japanese festivals. Typically, however, they did not know much about Japanese culture.

Later generations were much more likely to marry outside the group than their parents. About 10 percent of Nisei married a non-Japanese American, while about half the Sansei did. That was much higher than the rate for other Asian American groups. Many of the children born into these multiethnic marriages identified with their Japanese heritage only slightly.

Maintaining Connections

The children of more recent Japanese immigrants, however, lived in more of a mixed culture. Their parents often sent them to Japanese school as well as to regular public school. Where the Issei had stressed blending into U.S. society, Japanese immigrants who arrived after World War II wanted their children to have more knowledge and awareness of Japanese culture. Many parents from this group tried to help their children keep in touch with their Japanese heritage—and relatives—by taking them back to Japan every few years. Children of today's immigrants may live an English-speaking, American-style life away from home and a more traditional Japanese life at home.

"I cannot communicate in this country. That is why I feel it is important that my children speak Japanese. So they can talk to me and my family. Speaking English is important so they can communicate with Americans. I speak Japanese with my children. This is important because my parents and my husband's parents are still in Japan, and I hope my children can communicate with them."

Setsuko K., Japanese-born woman who came to the United States in the 1970s

Japanese Americans in U.S. Society

The 2000 Census counted about 1.15 million Japanese Americans living in the United States. They were the sixth largest Asian American group, after Chinese, Filipinos, Asian Indians, Koreans, and Vietnamese. Although in 1970, Japanese Americans had been the largest Asian American group, their current ranking shows that the Japanese American community is growing much more slowly than other Asian American groups. Two reasons account for this decline. One is that the immigration rate among other Asian groups is now much higher. The other is that Japanese American families have relatively few children.

Today's Japanese Americans

Today, among Japanese Americans who were raised in the United States, more than 30 percent of men and more than 40 percent of women have non-Japanese spouses. Reflecting this fact, nearly one-third of all Japanese Americans trace their heritage to at least one group other than Japanese. Only about two out of every five Japanese Americans speak Japanese at home.

Just under half of all Japanese Americans live in California and Hawaii, the two states that have traditionally been the main areas of settlement. In Hawaii, Japanese Americans comprise about 24 percent of the population. Many of the "Japantowns" that existed in West Coast cities before World War II have disappeared, but strong Japanese American communities still exist in California—notably in Los Angeles and San Francisco.

Religion Among Japanese Americans

Before World War II, most Japanese Americans were Buddhists. Today, the majority of Japanese Americans who practice religion are Christians. Traditionally, however, Japanese people are flexible

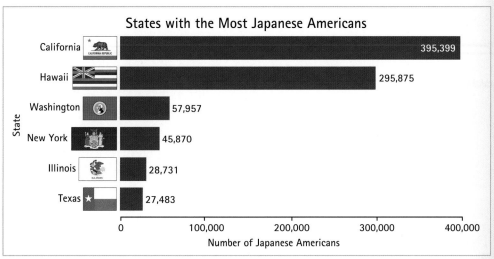

States with the Most Japanese Americans

State	Number of Japanese Americans
California	395,399
Hawaii	295,875
Washington	57,957
New York	45,870
Illinois	28,731
Texas	27,483

Number of Japanese Americans

Source: U.S. Census Bureau, Census 2000

▲ The largest Japanese American population is in California. Hawaii has the highest percentage of Japanese Americans, however.

about religion—a wedding ceremony may be Shinto, for example, while a funeral would be Buddhist. Japanese Americans may follow both Christian and Buddhist practices. Many Japanese American Buddhist temples in the United States have taken on Western aspects, such as running Sunday schools and acting as social centers for the community.

Success in Society

From the beginning, Japanese Americans have made a contribution to U.S. society. Sugarcane workers helped build Hawaii's economy in the late 1800s and early 1900s. Japanese American farmers contributed to the growth of California's agricultural industry.

For many decades, despite the prejudice and hardships Japanese Americans faced, they adapted remarkably well to U.S. culture and thrived as an ethnic community. The idea of Japanese American success is now considered a stereotype, but Japanese Americans have undoubtedly built an impressive educational record. By 2000, more than half of all U.S.-born Japanese Americans had a college degree. This rate of college graduation is slightly higher than for Asian Americans as a whole. In contrast, fewer than 30 percent of white Americans had such a degree.

Just over half of all Japanese Americans work in higher-level careers, such as professions, technical careers, and management. This, too, is higher than the rate for white Americans, which is about 38 percent, and for Asian Americans as a whole (45 percent). Family incomes tend to be higher than those of white Americans and other Asian Americans. The share of Japanese Americans living in poverty is lower than among other Asian groups.

Celebrating Japanese Heritage

Japanese Americans suffered a deep hurt because of the World War II internment. Even today, many Japanese Americans can describe occasions when they have been

"[Obon in the United States] reveals for all to see what remains of the old culture, what's in it that is still valued because it can still nourish and enrich us, and how much of it has taken root in its new environment to become something new yet familiar."

The Reverend Mas Kodani of Los Angeles' Senshin Buddhist Temple talking about the celebration of the Japanese tradition of Obon, quoted by Annie Nakao, San Francisco Chronicle, *2005*

Holidays and Festivals

A number of events in the United States celebrate the heritage of Japanese Americans. The Japanese tradition of celebrating the blossoming of cherry trees in spring was brought to Washington, D.C., in 1912, where the National Cherry Blossom Festival still takes place. The event includes a parade, a street festival, and many other activities. Today, there are cherry blossom festivals in several states, including Georgia, New York, Alabama, Michigan, California, and Washington.

Small and large communities across the United States observe Obon—an ancient Buddhist tradition honoring the spirits of ancestors—that is a major holiday in Japan. The first American celebration of Obon took place in Hawaii in 1910. The Japanese New Year is another important celebration that lasts for three days starting January 1. Many Japanese American families cook and eat traditional dishes, play games, and observe rituals for New Year.

Every year, Los Angeles hosts Nisei Week, usually held in August. Nisei Week is a Japanese American tradition rather than a Japanese one. The weeklong celebration of all things Japanese and Japanese American dates back to 1934 and takes place in Little Tokyo, center of the Japanese American community in Los Angeles. Nisei Week includes a parade, a fashion show, sports tournaments, musical performances, a ball, and many other events.

▲ Obon is an important Japanese holiday celebrated in several Japanese American communities. A 2005 parade celebrating Obon in San Jose, California, featured traditional dancers and costumes.

insulted or discriminated against because of their ethnic identity. Their physical appearance still leads some white people to perceive Japanese Americans as something other than American.

To an extent, Japanese Americans reacted to discrimination by denying the Japanese part of their heritage in order to try to gain acceptance. Japanese American communities and cultural organizations, however, have managed to maintain some Japanese traditions, and these have flourished in recent years.

Japanese food has become very popular in the last few decades, and restaurants serving the traditional fish dishes of sushi and sashimi have enjoyed great success in cities across the country. The Japanese art of paper folding—called origami—and Japanese-style gardening have also become well known. Japanese music, theater, and dance are performed across the nation. Americans

in all states practice Japanese martial arts, including karate, judo, and aikido.

Japanese American Contributions

Japanese Americans have made many contributions in literature and other arts, in science, and in sports. Ronald Takaki, a university professor, wrote groundbreaking histories of the experiences of Asian Americans. Another professor, the physicist Michio Kaku, helped develop the string field theory, a revolutionary way of looking at the universe.

◀ Kristi Yamaguchi skates at the Winter Olympics in France in 1992, where she won a gold medal for the United States.

"Please remember that the story of my experiences during World War II is—by itself—not important. Much more significant are the values that the 442nd Regimental Combat Team and other segregated units represented: that patriotism and love of our great country are not limited to any ethnic group, and wartime hysteria must never again lead us to trample on our democratic principles."

Senator Daniel Inouye, who lost his arm fighting in World War II with the 442nd Regimental Combat Team, in a letter to a young visitor to his office, 2003

▲ Daniel Inouye, war hero and one of the longest-serving U.S. senators in history, tours the National Japanese American Memorial to Patriotism in Washington, D.C., on its opening day in June 2001.

In the sports field, Apolo Anton Ohno thrilled millions of Americans with his skill in short-track speed skating. Figure skater Kristi Yamaguchi charmed millions of Americans with her grace.

Many thousands of Japanese Americans have made other, less noticeable achievements. These ordinary people have not gained fame or been awarded honors. They have simply worked hard and honestly in the effort to build better lives for their children and to make the United States a better place to live—a place that would accept them as valuable and equal members. In more than one hundred years of history, Japanese Americans have endured hardships and harsh treatment. Traditional values of perseverance and duty to the community have enabled them to endure and overcome huge difficulties. Over the years, Japanese Americans have accomplished a great deal in U.S. society.

Notable Japanese Americans

Tetsuya Fujita (1920–1998) Japanese-born scientist who came to United States in 1953 to study meteorology and whose work led to the installation of weather-related radar at airports.

Samuel Ichiye Hayakawa (1906–1992) Canadian-born scholar and politician who came to the United States as a teacher and later served as president of San Francisco State College and as a U.S. senator.

Daniel Inouye (1924–) Hawaiian-born politician who joined the 442nd Regimental Combat Team at age eighteen and won several medals for bravery during World War II, was elected to the House of Representatives in 1959, and has served in the U.S. Senate since 1963.

Michio Kaku (1947–) U.S.-born physicist and science writer who became co-creator of the string field theory and professor of theoretical physics at the City University of New York.

Yuri Kochiyama (1922–) U.S.-born political activist who campaigned for civil rights and sought unity for Asian Americans with other ethnic groups.

Norman Yoshio Mineta (1931–) U.S.-born politician and internee during World War II, joined the U.S Army, and after a distinguished career in Congress, became the U.S. Secretary of Commerce in 2000 and the U.S. Secretary of Transportation in 2001.

Isamu Noguchi (1904–1988) U.S.-born sculptor and designer who created designs in many fields, including park landscaping design and furniture.

Seiji Ozawa (1935–) Classical music conductor who was born in China of Japanese parents, trained as a pianist, and worked as the musical director of the Boston Symphony Orchestra for nearly thirty years.

Eric Ken Shinseki (1942–) Hawaiian-born army general who graduated from the United States Military Academy in 1965, served in Vietnam, and became the thirty-fourth Chief of Staff of the United States Army, serving from 1999 to 2003.

Kristi Yamaguchi (1971–) Japanese American figure skater who began figure skating before age ten and won the women's singles figure skating gold medal in 1992 Winter Olympic Games.

Minoru Yamasaki (1912–1986) Nisei architect who was born in Washington and whose most famous design was New York City's World Trade Center twin towers, destroyed in 2001.

Time Line

1853   Matthew Perry demands that Japan agree to trade and contact with the United States.

1885   Japanese government lifts its ban on emigration.

1898   United States takes possession of Hawaii.

1900   Congress passes Organic Act, putting Hawaii under U.S. law and making labor contracts illegal.

1908   Gentlemen's Agreement ends immigration of Japanese workers; Japanese Association of America is formed.

1910   Angel Island immigration station opens in San Francisco Bay, California.

1913   California passes first of the alien land laws.

1920   Japan stops issuing passports to Japanese women.

1922   U.S. Supreme Court rules that Japanese cannot become U.S. citizens; Congress passes Cable Act, which revoked the U.S. citizenship of American women who married aliens ineligible for citizenship.

1924   National Origins Act bars immigration of aliens ineligible for citizenship.

1941   United States and Japan go to war.

1942   Internment begins of Japanese Americans living on the West Coast.

1943   Japanese American 442nd Regimental Combat Team is formed within the U.S. Army.

1944   Supreme Court upholds legality of internment, then rules that loyal Japanese American U.S. citizens cannot be held in camps.

1945   World War II ends; most Japanese Americans are allowed to return home.

1947   United States allows Japanese military brides to enter the United States.

1948   Supreme Court weakens alien land laws; Congress passes law allowing Japanese Americans to file claims for property lost due to internment.

1952   California Supreme Court rules that alien land laws are unconstitutional; McCarran-Walter Act makes citizenship available to Issei and allows a small number of Japanese to immigrate.

1959   Daniel Inouye becomes first Japanese American member of Congress.

1967   Supreme Court rules that bans on interracial marriages are unconstitutional.

1988   Congress passes Civil Liberties Act of 1988.

1992   Kristi Yamaguchi wins gold medal in figure skating for the United States at the Winter Olympic Games in Albertville, France.

1999   General Eric Shinseki becomes Chief of Staff of the U.S. Army.

2000   Norman Mineta becomes U.S. Secretary of Commerce and the first Asian American to join the Cabinet.

Glossary

alien person living in a nation other than his or her birth nation and who has not become a citizen of his or her new nation of residence.

barracks shed-like buildings used for temporary or military housing

census official population count

civilian person who is not a member of the armed forces

culture language, beliefs, customs, and ways of life shared by a group of people from the same region or nation

detention holding in custody. People held in this way are called detainees.

discrimination treatment of one group or person differently from another

embargo law that blocks trade with another nation

emigrate leave one nation or region to go and live in another place

ethnic having certain racial, national, tribal, religious, or cultural origins

evacuated removed from homes in times of danger

feudal system society in which a few people own large areas of land and control the lives of the people who work that land

heritage something handed down from previous generations

immigrant person who arrives in a new nation or region to take up residence

interest additional charge that someone who borrows money must pay to the lender

internment camp place where people are confined, usually during wartime

Issei people born in Japan who immigrated to the United States and became the first generation of Japanese Americans

Kibei Japanese Americans born in the United States and educated in Japan

kimono long, wide-sleeved robe worn by both male and female Japanese

lease contract giving the right to a piece of land for a set period of time

naturalization process of becoming a citizen by living in the United States for a number of years and passing a citizenship test

Nikkei people of Japanese descent living in a country other than Japan

Nisei children born in the United States of Issei parents

plantation large farm that grows primarily one crop, such as sugarcane, cotton, or tea

prejudice bias against or dislike of a person or group because of race, nationality, or other factors

redress compensation for something that was wrong or unfair

ritual action that follows a set pattern and has a special, often religious, meaning

Sansei children of the Nisei and grandchildren of the Issei

segregated separated into different ethnic or racial groups

stereotype image, often incorrect, that people have of certain groups

visa document that permits a person to enter a nation for a set period of time

Yonsei children of the Sansei and great-grandchildren of the Issei

Further Resources

Books

Asakawa, Gil. *Being Japanese American: A Sourcebook for Nikkei, Hapa . . . and Their Friends*. Stone Bridge Press, 2004.

Ganeri, Anita. *Buddhism*. Religions of the World (series). World Almanac® Library, 2000.

Hoobler, Dorothy, and Thomas Hoobler. *The Japanese American Family Album*. American Family Albums (series). Oxford University Press, 1998.

Houston, Jeanne Wakatsuki, and James D. Houston. *Farewell to Manzanar: A True Story of Japanese American Experience During and After the World War II Internment*. Houghton Mifflin, 2002.

Web Sites

A History of Japanese Americans in California
www.cr.nps.gov/history/online_books/5views/5views4.htm
National Park Service Web site about the early history of Japanese Americans

Nikkei Resources—Discover Nikkei
www.discovernikkei.org/en/resources/
A wealth of Nikkei information coordinated by the Japanese American National Museum

Publisher's note to educators and parents: Our editors have carefully reviewed these Web sites to ensure that they are suitable for children. Many Web sites change frequently, however, and we cannot guarantee that a site's future contents will continue to meet our high standards of quality and educational value. Be advised that children should be closely supervised whenever they access the Internet.

Where to Visit

Japanese American National Museum
369 East First Street; Los Angeles, CA 90012.
Telephone: (213) 625-0414; *www.janm.org*

About the Author

Dale Anderson studied history and literature at Harvard University in Cambridge, Massachusetts. He lives in Newtown, Pennsylvania, where he writes and edits educational books. Anderson has written many books for young people, including a history of Ellis Island, published by World Almanac® Library in its *Landmark Events in American History* series.

Index